Contents

Cathy Lawday

Snick and Snack written by Paul Shipton

Course consultants: Julie Ashworth and John Clark

Oxford University Press
1999

Listen and point

I live in a small house.

There's 1 room.

I live in a castle.
There are 145 rooms.

Listen and choose

Listen, point and repeat

Listen and do

Listen and say

quiz

film

wildlife programme

sports programme

cartoon

music programme

Pair work

Sing

TV Every Day

At five o'clock on Monday,
On Tuesday at three,
On Wednesday at six o'clock,
I watch TV.

At two o'clock on Thursday,
On Friday at ten,
On Saturday and Sunday,
I watch TV again.

My mum and dad and teacher say,
'Don't watch TV every day!'
But still I watch and still I stare,
Oh, no. LOOK! My eyes are square!

Listen and follow

Pair work

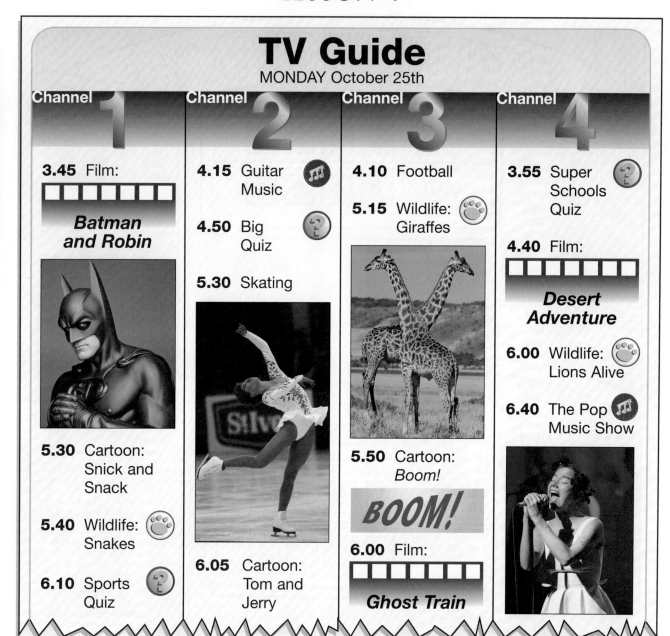

TV Guide
MONDAY October 25th

Channel 1

3.45 Film:

Batman and Robin

5.30 Cartoon: Snick and Snack

5.40 Wildlife: Snakes

6.10 Sports Quiz

Channel 2

4.15 Guitar Music

4.50 Big Quiz

5.30 Skating

6.05 Cartoon: Tom and Jerry

Channel 3

4.10 Football

5.15 Wildlife: Giraffes

5.50 Cartoon: *Boom!*

BOOM!

6.00 Film:

Ghost Train

Channel 4

3.55 Super Schools Quiz

4.40 Film:

Desert Adventure

6.00 Wildlife: Lions Alive

6.40 The Pop Music Show

Read

Listen. True or false?

Listen and say

AB 61

Play the game

Pair work

It's on Channel 1. It's at 5.40. What is it?

It's a wildlife programme.

7

Listen

Listen and answer

Play the game

My TV Chart

On Monday I watch a sports quiz. It's on Channel 1 at 6.10. On Tuesday I watch ...

MONDAY 6·10	Channel 1 sports quiz
TUESDAY 6·00	Channel 2 Tom and Jerry
WEDNESDAY ____	____
THURSDAY 6·45	Channel 4 sport
FRIDAY ____	____
SATURDAY 2·30	Channel 3 tennis
SUNDAY 5·25	Channel 1 film

Listen and repeat

Talk about your TV chart

PASSWORDS RHYME

The **witch** is on the **chimney**, playing **chess** and eating **chips**.
The **fish** is in the **shower**, washing **dishes** and **ships**.

Listen and repeat

Say the rhyme

SNACK SNICK GRANNY TIBS

1 Listen, Snick. It's time for my favourite music programme on the radio.

Oh, Snack!

2 Wait a minute. Radio?... I've got an idea.

3 Twenty minutes later...

SALLY'S TV and RADIO SHOP

Put these on, Snack.

4 Tibs, it's 3.15. It's time for my favourite exercise programme.

5 Jump three times! Now turn right!

What have the wolves got now? Hmm...Where's our radio?

6 Go through the window!

7 I'm in the bathroom.

8 OK, Snack...

...Find the stairs!

Yes, Snick.

9 Touch your toes...

OK... Now!

CLICK!

27

Listen and choose

A

B

C

28

Listen and point

Say the rhyme

January	February	March	April
May	June	July	August
September	October	November	December

Say the months and clap your hands.
Say the months as fast as you can!

30

Listen and read

Listen and answer

Listen, point and say

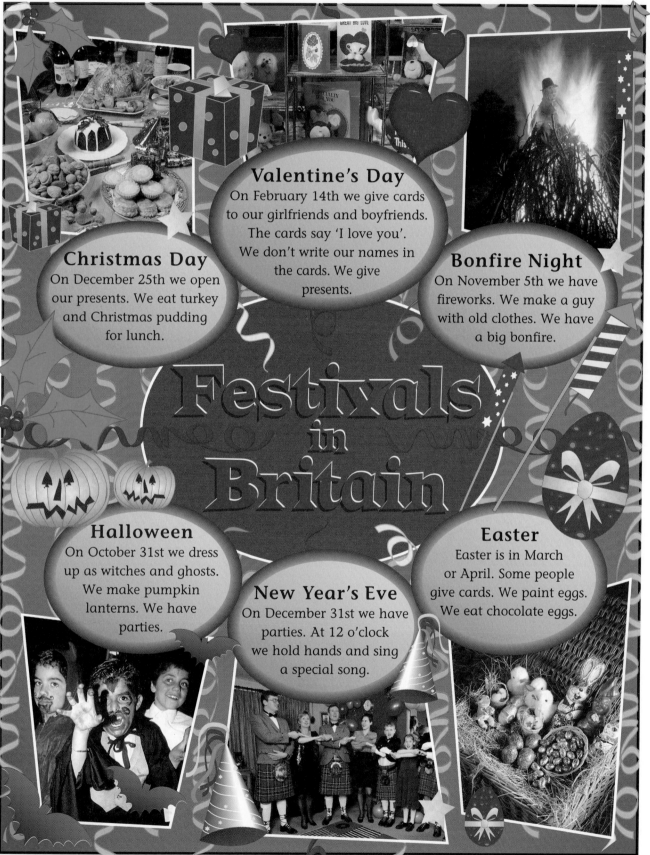

Valentine's Day
On February 14th we give cards to our girlfriends and boyfriends. The cards say 'I love you'. We don't write our names in the cards. We give presents.

Christmas Day
On December 25th we open our presents. We eat turkey and Christmas pudding for lunch.

Bonfire Night
On November 5th we have fireworks. We make a guy with old clothes. We have a big bonfire.

Festivals in Britain

Halloween
On October 31st we dress up as witches and ghosts. We make pumpkin lanterns. We have parties.

New Year's Eve
On December 31st we have parties. At 12 o'clock we hold hands and sing a special song.

Easter
Easter is in March or April. Some people give cards. We paint eggs. We eat chocolate eggs.

Sing

A Party

Let's have a party, a party, a party,
Let's have a birthday party today.
With balloons and presents, and a cake with candles,
Let's have a birthday party today.

Let's have a party, a party, a party,
Let's have a Christmas party today.
With a tree and crackers, and cards and presents,
Let's have a Christmas party today.

Let's have a party, a party, a party,
Let's have a Halloween party today.
With ghosts and witches, and pumpkin lanterns,
Let's have a Halloween party today.

Let's have a party, a party, a party,
Let's have a party EVERY day!

PM 10

Play

BINGO

LESSON 4

1. Friday is October the 31st. Let's have a Halloween party.
2. Yes! Let's dress up as ghosts and witches. Let's paint our faces too!
3. Let's have balloons! And play games!
4. Let's make pumpkin lanterns.
5. Yes, and let's decorate the house.
6. Let's eat pizzas and let's eat ice-cream too!
7. It's a great idea! Let's write the invitations now!

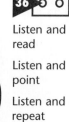

36

Listen and read

Listen and point

Listen and repeat

a

b

c

d

Please come to a

HALLOWEEN PARTY!

on: Friday October 31st

at: 7.15

at: 10, Pear Tree Road

e

Play the game

My Festivals Calendar

This is my festivals calendar.
February the 14th is a festival.
It's Valentine's Day.
May the 1st is May Day.
June the 24th is Saint John's Day.

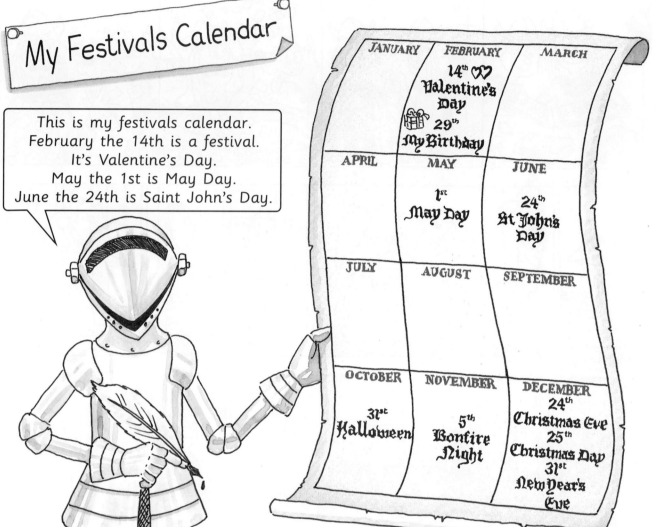

JANUARY	FEBRUARY	MARCH
	14th ♡ Valentine's Day 29th My Birthday	
APRIL	MAY	JUNE
	1st May Day	24th St John's Day
JULY	AUGUST	SEPTEMBER
OCTOBER	NOVEMBER	DECEMBER
31st Halloween	5th Bonfire Night	24th Christmas Eve 25th Christmas Day 31st New Year's Eve

40
Listen and repeat

AB 15
Talk about your festivals calendar

PASSWORDS RHYME

I like **g**ymnastics and ba**dg**es and **j**udo.
You like **y**oga and **y**oghurt and **y**o-**y**os.

41
Listen and repeat

Say the rhyme

LESSON 1

44

Listen and choose

45

Listen, point and repeat

Listen and say

coin

postcard

sticker

keyring

doll

badge

UNIT 3
LESSON 2

I collect coins and stickers.
Simon

I collect badges and dolls.
Helen

I collect badges and stickers.
Jack

I collect postcards and keyrings.
Sarah

I collect dolls, keyrings, and coins.
Aisha

I collect badges, coins, and postcards.
Lee

 47

Listen and point

Listen and repeat

Listen and answer

Pair work

Listen and point

Listen and repeat

the USA
Spain
Morocco
France
Britain
Italy
Argentina

Match

Pair work

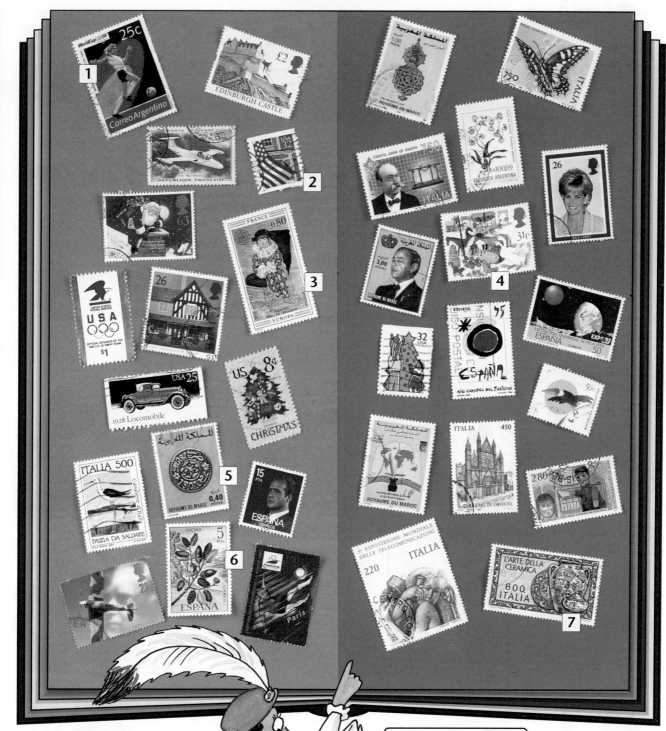

52 Listen and point

Listen and answer

Pair work

Play I-Spy

AB 52

Where's this stamp from?

It's from Italy.

Say the rhyme

RHYME

My Collection

Collecting, collecting. I like collecting.
What have I got in my collection?

I've got a **stamp** from Argentina,
I've got a **stamp** from France,
I've got a **stamp** from Italy,
And a **stamp** from Spain.

Collecting, collecting. Do you like collecting?
What have you got in your collection?

Listen and choose

Pair work

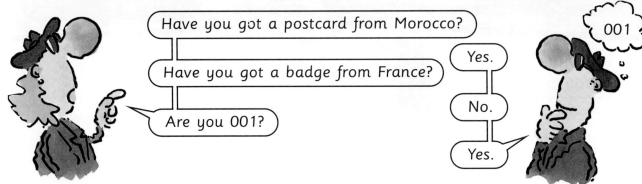

My Collections Cards

Here are my collections cards.
This stamp is from Italy.
It's got a pizza on it.
This stamp is from France.
It's got a croissant on it...

59

Listen and repeat

AB 21

AB 63 AB 65

Talk about your collections cards

Play the collections game

PASSWORDS RHYME

For lunch I want chillies and cherries and cheese,
Jelly and cabbage and a jug of juice, please.

60

Listen and repeat

Say the rhyme

1

Hi, Snick.

WAAGH! A ghost!

2

Sorry, Snick. But it's October the 31st today.

3

HALLOWEEN PARTY TONIGHT

Look at Granny's house. I love Halloween.

Oh, Snack!

4

Wait a minute! Where's **my** ghost costume?

Here it is. Er... Why?

5

Help! Ghosts! AAAAaa!

I've got an idea.

6

I love parties, Tibs. Now where's my hat?

Come to Granny's Halloween Party at 8 o'clock

7

Hmm. They're not ghosts. They're wolves.

8

The door is open. Come on, Snack!

9

The room is empty.

Where's Granny? I'm hungry.

24

63

Listen and choose

64

Listen and do

Listen and repeat

Say the rhyme

Swim and jump and run and hop.
Eat and drink and sleep, and then,
Swim and jump and run. Don't stop!
Eat and drink and sleep again!

There was an Old Woman

66
Listen to
the story

Story Time

67
Listen, point
and repeat

Listen and
do

Listen and
say

 a spider

 a fly

 a cow

 a bird

 a horse

 a goat

 a cat

 a dog

Listen and read

Listen and say

Listen. True or false?

Fantastic animal facts

They live for ...

70 years

50 years

14 years

10 years

Elephants live in Africa and Asia. They drink 90 litres of water a day and eat 160 kilos of grass, leaves, and fruit. They eat for 20 hours a day. Elephants like to play in water.

Koalas live in Australia. They live in eucalyptus trees. They only eat eucalyptus leaves. Baby koalas live in a pouch on their mother's body for six months. Then they ride on her back for six months.

Gorillas live in Africa. They are 2 metres tall. They sleep in nests in trees and they make a new nest every day. Gorillas don't eat meat. They eat leaves and fruit.

Anteaters live in South America. They haven't got teeth. They've got a long, sticky tongue – 60 centimetres long! Anteaters eat ants and other insects. They eat 30,000 ants every day! Baby anteaters ride on their mother's back for two years.

They sleep for ...

4 hours

12 hours

22 hours

71

Listen and correct

Listen and answer

Pair work

AB 52

LESSON 5

Sing

SONG

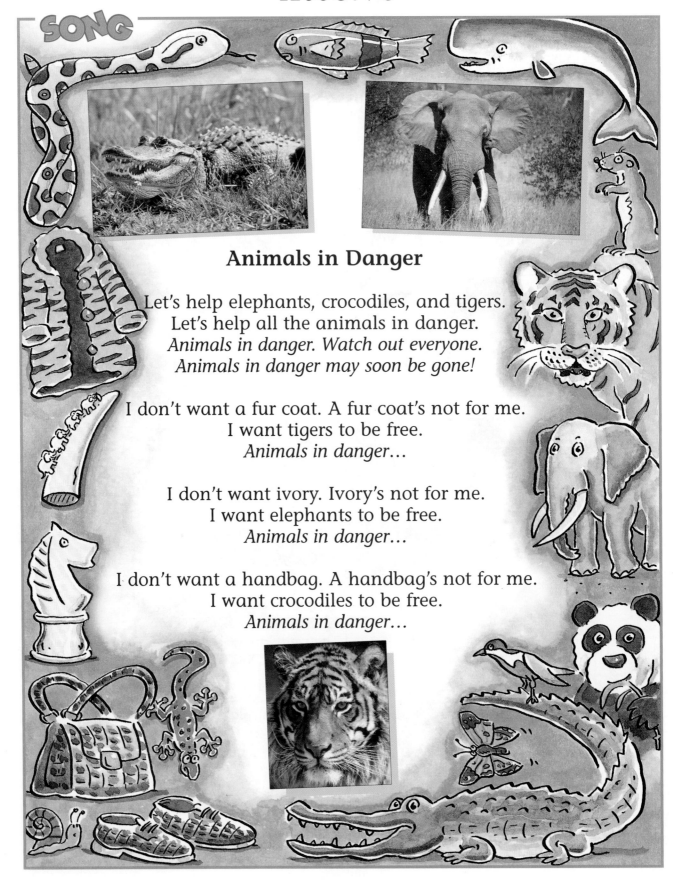

Animals in Danger

Let's help elephants, crocodiles, and tigers.
Let's help all the animals in danger.
Animals in danger. Watch out everyone.
Animals in danger may soon be gone!

I don't want a fur coat. A fur coat's not for me.
I want tigers to be free.
Animals in danger…

I don't want ivory. Ivory's not for me.
I want elephants to be free.
Animals in danger…

I don't want a handbag. A handbag's not for me.
I want crocodiles to be free.
Animals in danger…

Listen and repeat

AB 27
Talk about your animal

My Animal Card

These animals live in Africa.

These animals live in Africa. They live in grassland. They eat meat. They eat zebras and deer. They drink water. They sleep for 20 hours a day. They live for 25 years. What are they?

Lions!

PASSWORDS RHYME

I've got a cot and a mop and a sock with spots.
I've got a comb and a bone and a rope with knots.

Listen and repeat

Say the rhyme

79

Listen and choose

B

C

80

Listen, point and do

Listen and repeat

PM 10

Play

BINGO

play tennis

play rugby

skate

skateboard

do gymnastics

do judo

dive

cycle

Can you play rugby?

Yes, I can.

82

Listen, point and repeat

Listen and answer

Pair work

SONG

83

Sing

I can do it!

I can cycle. I can skateboard.
I can swim and skate and ski.
I can play tennis. I can play rugby.
I can play basketball.
Look at me!

I can dive and do judo.
I can jump and I can throw.
I can skip and hop together.
I can do it.
Look. Oh, no!

Listen and read

Listen. True or false?

AB 67 ✂

Play the game

Star ★ File

1 This is Denise Lewis. She's an athlete. Her birthday is August 27th. Denise can do the heptathlon. The heptathlon has seven different events.

2 Denise can jump 6.7 metres in the long jump and she can jump 1.8 metres in the high jump.

3 She can throw the javelin 56 metres and the shot 14 metres. The shot weighs 4 kilos! Denise can run the 100 metres hurdles in 14 seconds. She can run 200 metres in 25 seconds and 800 metres in 2 minutes, 17 seconds.

4 Her favourite event is the long jump. She doesn't like the 800 metres very much.

5 Denise has got a silver medal from the World Championships in Athens in 1997 and lots of other medals.

Heptathlon (women)
- 100 metres hurdles
- shot
- high jump
- long jump
- 200 metres
- javelin
- 800 metres

LESSON 4

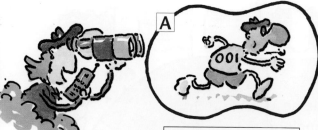

A — He's running.

B — He's swimming.

C — He's cycling.

88 ○ ○
Listen, point and repeat

Listen and say

89 ○ ○
Listen, point and repeat

Listen and answer

Listen and correct

3 metres

Is 004 swimming?

False.

Yes.

Pair work

LESSON 5

Play the game

My Sports Challenge

Can you jump 1 metre?

94 🔊

Listen and repeat

AB 33

Do the sports challenge with a partner

SPORTS CHALLENGE

Can you jump 1 metre?

Can you throw a ball 10 metres?

Can you hop 25 metres in 15 seconds?

Can you cycle 200 metres in 10 seconds?

Can you skip and hop?

Can you skate and play tennis at the same time?

Can you run and sing at the same time?

PASSWORDS RHYME

95 🔊

Listen and repeat

Say the rhyme

In the bank there's a cat with a hat and a map.
In the park there's a shark with a scarf and a cap.

38

Stop! Stand here!

But what about the bull?

Now jump!

I can't jump! I can't move my feet!

Er... Captain, two wolves are flying past the window!

Don't be silly! Wolves can't fly.

?!

Next week on Animal Hour we go to Africa to see the amazing birds of...

I can see two amazing birds now!

98
Listen and
choose

99
Listen, point
and repeat

Listen and
say

Say the
rhyme

It's Saturday today. Let's go to the zoo.
Let's go to the park and the restaurant too.
Let's go to the library. Let's go to the pool.
Let's go to the shops. Let's NOT go to school!

LESSON 2

Listen to
the story

Story Time

Lady Daly and the Thief

museum

library

fire station

police station

Listen, point
and repeat

AB
69

Listen and
play

market

bank

church

cinema

LESSON 3

Turn left.

Turn right.

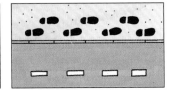
Go along the road.

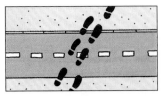
Go across the road.

106 ⊙ ○

Listen and
answer

Pair work

Listen and
follow

AB
52

Where's Molly?

At the ...

Olly   Billy   Barry   Molly   Milly   Sally

Say the rap

Road Safety Rap

Left, right, one, two, three.
Say the Road Safety Rap with me.

Stop at the road. Listen carefully.
Is anything coming? What can you see?
Look left. Look right. Get ready to go.
Is anything coming, fast or slow?
Don't run. Walk across the road.
Don't forget the Safety Code.

Left, right, one, two, three.
Say the Road Safety Rap with me.

LESSON 5

Listen and read

Listen. True or false?

Listen and answer

Jorvik was a Viking town in England. There were 10,000 people in Jorvik. There were roads and houses.

There were toilets. There were pigs, chickens, and sheep too.

There was a market with many stalls and workshops. There were cloth shops, jewellery shops, leather shops, fish shops, and shoe shops.

YORK - now

Now Jorvik is called York and there are over 100,000 people. There are houses, cinemas, churches, schools, banks, restaurants, and many shops. There is a police station and a library.

There are lots of cars, lorries, buses, and trains. There is an old wall round the town.

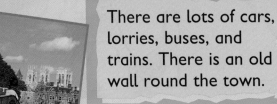

There are lots of tourists in York. They come to the Jorvik museum and learn about the Vikings.

My Poster

Come to Rocktown.
It's fantastic!
There's a museum.
There's a market.
There are lots of ...

COME TO
ROCKTOWN
IT'S FANTASTIC!

114
Listen and repeat

AB 39
Talk about your poster

PASSWORDS RHYME

The **h**orse is **dr**awing on the w**all** with **ch**alk,
A **cl**ou**d**, a **cl**ow**n**, a **t**ow**er**, and a **f**ork.

115
Listen and repeat

Say the rhyme

LESSON 1

117

Listen and choose

118

Listen, point and repeat

Say the rhyme

AB 71

Play the game

Shorts, shoes, coat, hat,
Jumper, jeans, and shirt.
Scarf, sandals, vest, cap,
T-shirt, dress, and skirt.

It's wet.

It's windy.

It's cold.

120

Listen and point

Listen and repeat

It's hot.

It's sunny.

It's cloudy.

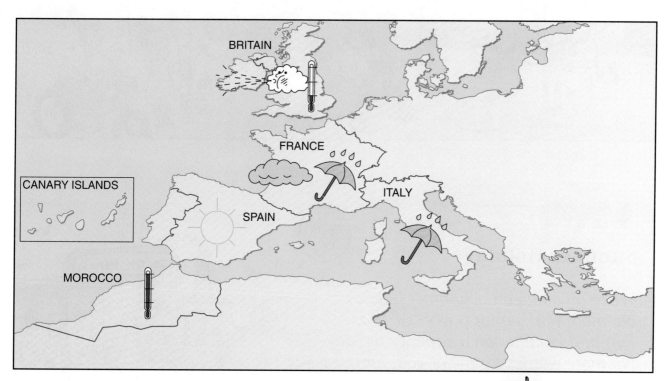

BRITAIN

FRANCE

CANARY ISLANDS

SPAIN

ITALY

MOROCCO

121

Listen. True or false?

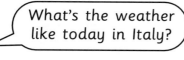

What's the weather like today in Italy?

It's wet.

Pair work

47

125

Listen, point
and repeat

Listen and
answer

AB
73

Play the
game

126

Sing

SONG

Summer Holiday

We're all going on a summer holiday.
No more working for a week or two.
Fun and laughter on a summer holiday,
No more worries for me or you, for a week or two.

We're going where the sun shines brightly.
We're going where the sea is blue.
We've seen it in the movies,
Now let's see if it's true.

We're all going on a summer holiday ...

Sarah

Simon

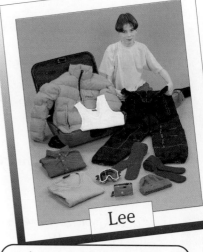

Lee

Aisha

Helen

Pair work

What's Helen packing?

She's packing a sun hat, a swimsuit, ...

Spain

Sun, sea, sand –
Superb Spain

a

b
France

ITALY

See Italy – Ski in Italy

c

A F R I C A

d

Visit historical London

e
England

49

132 Listen and read

Listen and match

Listen and correct

For my holiday last year I camped in Scotland. It was great! I cooked on the camp-fire. Mmm, delicious!

I walked in the mountains—fifteen kilometres!

I cycled on the beach. And I collected shells.

I played tennis.

I watched the fishing boats.

I listened to Scottish music, and I danced too!

I visited a castle. It was five hundred years old!

It was a wonderful holiday.

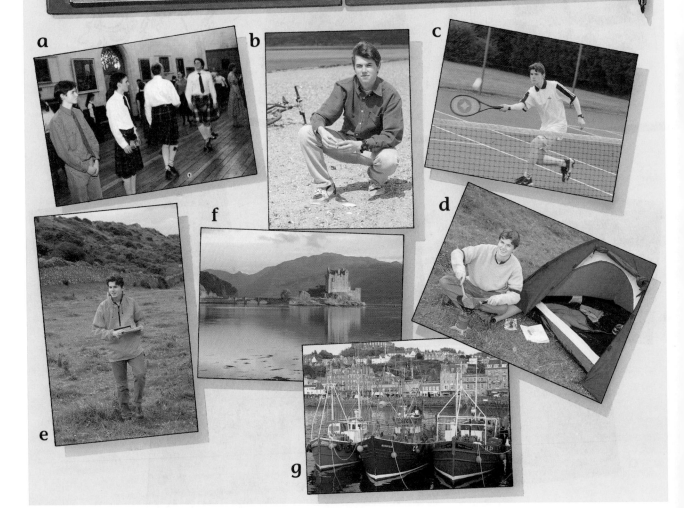

a

b

c

d

e

f

g

My Postcard

Dear Lance,
I'm on holiday in Italy.
It's hot and sunny.
I'm sitting on the beach.
I'm watching the boats
and I'm eating ice-cream.
I'm having a great time!
Love from Bess

134

Listen and repeat

AB 45

Read your postcard

PASSWORDS RHYME

The big mountain**eer** is riding a d**eer**.
He's got a b**ear**d and a sp**ear** and an **ear**ring in his **ear**.

135

Listen and repeat

Say the rhyme

SNACK SNICK

SNICK and SNACK

GRANNY TIBS

1 Look, Granny's packing. She's going on holiday.

2 This is great, Tibs. I love holidays!

Hmm. Where are those wolves?

THE BEACH 50 kilometres

3 Faster, Snack! Faster!

BEACH kilometres

Later...

4 Look! Granny's swimming.

5 Swimming? Wait! I've got an idea. Come on, Snack.

6 Wonderful! I love the beach!

Hmm. They're not fish.

7 It's time for dinner!

Er, Snick?

8 It's a shark! Aaargh!

Help!

LESSON 1

Listen and choose

Act

LESSON 2

141
Listen and follow

Pair work

SONG

142
Sing

Hello, Goodbye

You say 'yes', I say 'no'.
You say 'stop' and I say 'go, go, go'.
Oh, no. You say 'goodbye' and I say 'hello'.
'Hello, hello'. I don't know why you say 'goodbye', I say 'hello'.
'Hello, hello'. I don't know why you say 'goodbye', I say 'hello'.

I say 'high', you say 'low'.
You say 'why?' and I say 'I don't know'.
Oh, no. You say 'goodbye' and I say 'hello'.
'Hello, hello'. I don't know why you say 'goodbye', I say 'hello'...

Listen and read

Listen. True or false?

Dear Kids Club

My name's Simon. I'm 11 years old. I live in a flat in York. I've got a sister and a brother.
I collect coins, stickers, and stamps.
I like sport. I can do judo and I can play tennis and rugby.

I've got a dog called Barney and I've got lots of fish. This is a photo of me and Barney.
I like TV. Kids Club is my favourite programme. I watch it every Saturday. It's great!

From
Simon Smith

Kids Club
Fun Television
London

LESSON 4

Play

57

Point
Play I-Spy

Pair work

What's this?

What's she doing?

It's a ...

She's ...

My Poem

WELCOME HOME

My Home
My mum and dad.
My sister and brother.
My cat.
My diary.
Chicken for dinner.
My bedroom.
That's my home.
I love my home.

152
Listen and repeat

AB
51
Say your poem

PASSWORDS RHYME

I've got **a** magazine, **a** picture, and **a** lobster for my mother.
I've got **an** iron, **s**ome spaghetti, and **a** panda for my brother.

153
Listen and repeat

Say the rhyme

The Twelve Days of Christmas

On the first day of Christmas,
my true love gave to me,
a partridge in a pear tree.

On the second day of Christmas,
my true love gave to me,
two turtle doves,
and a partridge in a pear tree.

On the third day of Christmas,
my true love gave to me,
three French hens ...

On the fourth day of Christmas,
my true love gave to me,
four calling birds ...

On the fifth day of Christmas,
my true love gave to me,
five gold rings ...

On the sixth day of Christmas,
my true love gave to me,
six geese laying ...

On the seventh day of Christmas,
my true love gave to me,
seven swans swimming ...

On the eighth day of Christmas,
my true love gave to me,
eight maids milking ...

On the ninth day of Christmas,
my true love gave to me,
nine pipers piping ...

On the tenth day of Christmas,
my true love gave to me,
ten drummers drumming ...

On the eleventh day of Christmas,
my true love gave to me,
eleven ladies dancing ...

On the twelfth day of Christmas,
my true love gave to me,
twelve lords leaping ...

Listen
Act

Scene 1

CINDERELLA and the PRINCE

NARRATOR: Cinderella lived with her sisters.

SISTER 1: Hey! There's a roller disco at the 'Universal'.

SISTER 2: When?

SISTER 1: At 7 o'clock tonight!

SISTER 2: Let's go to the roller disco!

SISTER 1: Let's meet the film star, Rocky Stone!

SISTER 2: Cinderella! Wash my jeans!

SISTER 1: Cinderella! Iron my shirt!

SISTER 2: Cinderella! Clean my skates!

Scene 2

SISTER 1: I'm fantastic!

SISTER 2: No, you aren't.

SISTER 1: Yes, I am.

SISTER 2: No, you aren't.

CINDERELLA: Goodbye. Oh, I can skate, but I can't go to the roller disco.
Oh! What's happening?

MR MAGIC: Abracadabra, abracadoo. You can go to the disco too!

CINDERELLA: I can't go. I haven't got any skates.

MR MAGIC: Abracadabra, abracadoo.
Here are roller skates for you!

CINDERELLA: Wow! Thank you!

MR MAGIC: Abracadabra, abracadock.
You must come home at 12 o'clock!

Scene 3

SISTER 1: Hello, Rocky!
SISTER 2: Oh, hello.
SISTER 1: Let's skate, Rocky. I can skate.
SISTER 2: No, you can't.
SISTER 1: Yes, I can.
SISTER 2: No, you can't.
ROCKY: I can skate. Look!
SAM: Ow! Watch out!
ROCKY: I'm Rocky Stone! Get out of my way!

Scene 4

SAM: Ow. My foot!
CINDERELLA: Can I help you?
Take off your skate.
SAM: Thank you. What's your name?
CINDERELLA: Cinderella.
SAM: My name's Sam.
CINDERELLA: Oh no! It's 12 o'clock!
I must go home!
SAM: I can't walk. Let's go by taxi.
CINDERELLA: I can't. I haven't got any money.
SAM: It's OK. I've got lots of money.
I'm a prince.
CINDERELLA: Oh, a prince!

Scene 5

SISTER 1: I can skate!
SISTER 2: I can skate too!
ROCKY: I can skate! Aaaargh!
Move this skate out
of my way!

Scene 6

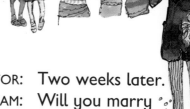

NARRATOR: Two weeks later.
SAM: Will you marry
me, Cinderella?
CINDERELLA: Yes!
NARRATOR: Cinderella married
the prince and
she was very happy.
ALL: 'Let's have a party,
a party, a party ...'

Oxford University Press, Great Clarendon Street,
Oxford OX2 6DP

Oxford   New York
Athens Auckland Bangkok Bogotá Buenos Aires
Calcutta Cape Town Chennai Dar es Salaam Delhi
Florence Hong Kong Istanbul Karachi Kuala Lumpur
Madrid Melbourne Mexico City Mumbai Nairobi
Paris São Paulo Singapore Taipei Tokyo Toronto
Warsaw

and associated companies in
Berlin Ibadan

OXFORD and OXFORD ENGLISH
are trade marks of Oxford University Press

ISBN 0 19 432149 5

© Oxford University Press 1999

First published 1999

No unauthorized photocopying

Printed in Hong Kong

Acknowledgements

Main Artists:
History Book Characters by: Pippa Sampson; The Snick and
Snack cartoon by: David Parkins; Spies by: Ian Dicks; 'There
was an Old Woman' story by: Adam Stower; 'Lady Daly and
the Thief' story by: Bill Dare Thorogood Illustration Agency;
Listening Puzzles by: Ollie Fowler; Songs, Raps, and Rhymes
by: Fred Pipes; 'Cinderella and the Prince' play by: Victor
Ambrus; 'The Twelve Days of Christmas' play by: Emma
Shaw-Smith Sylvie Poggio Agency

Other Artists:
Brett Breckon pp 44, 50, 56; Bill Dare Thorogood Illustration
Agency p 41 (bottom); Garry Davies pp 20 (top flags), 29, 42,
48 (top), 58; Ollie Fowler pp 6, 13, 28, 34, 55; Alan Rowe pp
8, 14 (bottom), 32 (bottom); Simon Smith pp 18 (bottom), 46
(bottom); Adam Stower p 27 (bottom); OUP Technical
Graphics pp 20 (bottom map),47(bottom map)

Commissioned Photography by:
Haddon Davies pp 13, 15, 19, 33, 49, 50, 56
Bill Osment p 13 (New Year)

**The publishers would like to thank the following for their
kind permission to reproduce photographs**
Allsport p 34 (G. Prior/Running/Shot putt, C. Brunskill/
Denise and flag/hurdles, G. Mortimore/Long jump, T. Duffy/
High jump); Alpha p 2 (Richard Chambury/Quiz show, Jeff
Spicer/ Damon Albarn/Blur), p 5 (Richard Chambury/Bjork);
Anthony Blake Photo Library p 13 (Gerrit Buntrock/Easter);
Ardea London Ltd p 28 (F. Gohier/Anteater); Britain on View
Photo Library p 44 (York Minster and walls); Capital Pictures
p 5 (George Clooney/Batman); Collections p 13 (Geoff
Howard/Christmas food, Brian Shuel/Valentine's day/
Bonfire), p 15 (Brian Shuel/Pumpkin), p 50 (F. Godwin/
Castle); Corbis p 47 (Beach); Edinburgh Photographic p 50
(Alex Gillespie/Oban harbour); Heather Angel/Biofotos p 2
(Lions); Leslie Garland Picture Library p 44 (Leslie Garland/
Stonegate, York/Jorvik sign); The Ronald Grant Archive p 2
(Tom and Jerry, Mars Attacks); Robert Harding p 13 (Robert
Frerck/Halloween), p 28 (Elephant), p 47 (M. Mawson/Rain,
P. Higgins/Winter, F. Hall/Storm clouds); Frank Lane Picture
Agency p 28 (Eric &David Hosking/Gorilla/Koala), p 47 (A.
Albinger/Wind, S. Moody Dembinsky/Sunshine);
Professional Sport International p 2 (Alex Livesey/Football), p
5 (Tommy Hindley/Skating); Telegraph Colour Library p 5
(Jonathan Scott/Giraffes), p 30 (John Downer/Tiger, Steve
Bloom/ Elephant, J. Brian Alker/Alligator); Travel Ink p 49
(Abbie Enock/Menorca, Steve Thompson/Austria, Ian
Booth/Alps,
I. MacFayden/Kenya, Ted Edwards/England).

**The publishers would like to thank the following for their
kind permission to reproduce songs**
Summer Holiday Words and music by Bruce Welch/Brian
Bennett (c) 1963 EMI Music Publishing trading as Elstree
Music, London, WC2H 0EA Reproduced by permission of IMP
Ltd; *There was an Old Woman who swallowed a fly* Rose
Bonne/Alan Mills (Copyright 1952 by Peer International
(Canada) Limited PeerMusic (UK) Ltd., 8-14 Verulam Street,
London WC1 Used by permission; Lyrics by John Lennon and
Paul McCartney, taken from the song *"Hello, Goodbye"* by
kind permission Sony/ATV Music Publishing Ltd.

The publishers wish to thank all the teachers who have
commented on the course at various stages of its
development.

Thank you to Robert Latham, Music Director, Bristol Schools
Chamber Choir for the actions to *The Twelve Days of Christmas*.